KINGFISHER
RIDING CLUB

HORSE & PONY
CARE

WRITTEN BY
Sandy Ransford

PHOTOGRAPHED BY
Bob Langrish

NEW YORK

Kingfisher would like to thank
The Talland School of Equitation,
Gloucestershire, England, and
Hartpury College, Gloucestershire,
England, for their invaluable help
in the production of this book.

Kingfisher

Larousse Kingfisher Chambers Inc.
80 Maiden Lane
New York, New York 10038
www.kingfisherpub.com

First published in 2002
10 9 8 7 6 5 4 3 2 1

ITR/0102/TWP/CG(CG)150SMA

LIBRARY OF CONGRESS
CATALOGING-IN-PUBLICATION DATA
has been applied for.

ISBN 0-7534-5439-4

Designed and edited by
BOOKWORK
Editor: Annabel Blackledge
Art Director: Jill Plank
Designer: Kate Mullins
Consultant: Nikki Herbert BHSI

For Kingfisher:
Editorial Director: Miranda Smith
Coordinating Editor: Denise Heal
Consultant: Lesley Ward
Art Director: Mike Davies
DTP Coordinator: Nicky Studdart
Production controller: Jo Blackmore

Printed in Singapore

Contents

Keeping
a pony

Keeping and caring for a pony is a serious commitment. It is hard work and takes up much of your time. It is also exciting, rewarding—and a lot of fun!

Providing company

Horses and ponies are herd animals and do not like being on their own. Ideally they should live with other horses and ponies, but if this is not possible, then the company of other animals can be substituted instead. If you have to keep a pony on its own, visit it frequently and make it feel a part of family life.

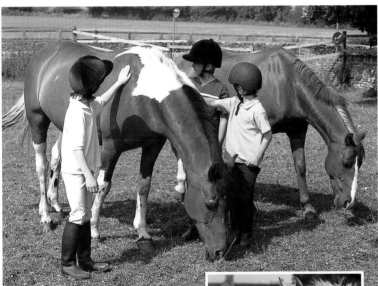

Human contact

Ponies like human company and will always appreciate your visits, though you may not be important enough to them to stop them from grazing! Be careful they do not tread on your feet as they walk forward. If you do offer treats, make sure there are enough to go around to all of the ponies in the group.

Ponies always enjoy a treat, but don't feed your pony treats every time you visit it because it will learn to expect them and might nip you.

Animal companionship

Once they get to know each other and realize they are part of a group that lives together, most animals become friends. Horses and ponies get on well with a variety of animals, from cats and dogs to livestock.

Although one horse or pony in a group is always dominant, two horses kept together usually become firm friends.

Horses and cats may enjoy each other's company, both in the stable or out in the pasture.

A friendly goat is good company for a lonely horse or pony, as are farm animals such as cattle and sheep.

Regular exercise

If a pony is kept in a stable, it has to be exercised every day. If it is not possible to ride it, then the pony should be turned out in a paddock for a while or lunged. Exercise keeps a pony healthy. Its circulation, heart, and lungs function better, and the bones and muscles are kept strong and healthy.

What a pony needs

A pony needs food and water, shelter from the weather, regular exercise, and companionship. In its natural state all these things are part of the life that it leads. But when we domesticate horses and ponies and make them work for us, they depend on us to fulfill all these needs. We owe it to them to do this as well as we possibly can.

Some form of shelter

A pony that lives in a pasture needs some kind of shelter from the sun and flies in the summer, and rain, wind, and snow in the winter. Trees and thick hedges provide a certain amount of protection, but a shelter built specifically for horses is the best solution, if it is possible.

Grazing in a pasture

Every pony should have access to good grazing for a part of each day. This is its natural way of life. Even if the grass is poor or during the winter, being out in the pasture allows your pony the freedom to move from place to place, roll, and occasionally gallop around, which helps keep it calm.

A suitable barn

If the pony is to be kept in a barn, or stabled, the building must meet certain requirements. The doorway should be high enough so the pony cannot bang its head. The stall should be well lit, with plenty of ventilation. It must have good drainage so that the bedding stays as dry as possible.

Feeding routine

A stabled pony needs regular feeding. The amount of food it needs depends on its individual needs and the amount of work it is being asked to do, but all stabled ponies need hay to replace the grass they would eat if they lived out in a pasture and grazed.

Bedding

The purpose of bedding is to provide a warm, dry, comfortable floor covering on which a horse or pony can lie down without knocking or injuring itself. It also takes some of the strain off the legs when a horse has to stand for long periods on a hard surface. Many different kinds are available. Whatever kind you choose, it should be at least 6 inches deep.

Straw is the dried stalks of wheat, barley, or oats. It is cheap to buy, but some ponies like eating it, and it can give them colic.

Hemp bedding is sold in vacuum-packed bales. It is useful for horses and ponies that have dust allergies, although it is expensive to buy.

Rubber matting is very expensive, but saves time on mucking out. You need to use some bedding on top of it to soak up any wetness.

Wood shavings are sold vacuum-packed. Any dust is extracted, so they are good for horses and ponies with breathing problems.

Shredded paper is cheap, but some ponies are allergic to the ink in it. It is heavy to lift and unpleasant to handle when it is wet.

Far to walk
You may have to carry a pasture-kept pony's tack some distance.

Ways to keep a pony

You can keep a pony out in a pasture, in a stable, or a combination of both. Looking after a stabled pony is hard work and takes up a lot of time. It also costs more than keeping a pony in a pasture, but it is very convenient. A pasture-kept pony requires less looking after, but preparing it for riding takes longer. Many people think the ideal system is to put ponies in a barn at night in the winter and during the day in the summer, and let them live outdoors the rest of the time.

Winter pasture

In the winter pastures can become very muddy, and your pony may be wet and dirty most of the time. This is bad for its feet and legs. But pasture-kept ponies are less likely to suffer from coughs and breathing problems than stabled ponies.

Preparing for a ride

It is easy to prepare a stabled pony for riding. But before you can ride a pasture-kept pony you must walk to the pasture, catch it, and then get it clean enough to tack up.

Catching a pony

Some ponies are difficult to catch, and some may try to pull away once caught. A trailing rope can be dangerous, so try not to let it go. It may be better to lead a difficult pony in a bridle.

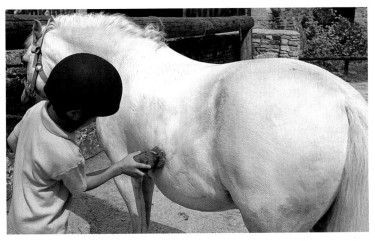

Regular feeding routine

When ponies are stabled, they need feeding at regular times. Whether or not they have concentrated feed (page 25), they need hay several times a day, either loose or in a haynet, to give them the bulk food that grazing would provide if they lived outdoors.

Mucking out

When a pony is stabled, you have to muck out the stall thoroughly at least once a day, as well as removing droppings at regular intervals. This takes time, and it can be very hard work.

A stabled pony is entirely dependent on you for food and water.

Removing mud and stains

A stabled pony needs just a quick brush over before and after exercise to make it look presentable. With a pasture-kept pony, you have to remove all the mud stuck to its coat. It is especially important to remove mud where the tack fits, or it may rub and cause sores.

Carrying water to the pasture

If the pasture does not have a trough that fills automatically, you will have to carry fresh water to it every day. In warm weather, and if there are several ponies in the pasture, this can mean many trips back and forth with buckets.

Stables

A long barn that is divided into box stalls with a central aisle is called an American barn. It is convenient in bad weather, but there can be problems with ventilation.

Where to keep a pony

If you are a new owner, it is a good idea to keep your pony at a boarding barn where you will have knowledgeable people to help you. Types of barns and their fees vary. Some boarding barns charge less if they can use your pony for lessons. You may be able to rent a pasture and stall from a farmer, or be lucky enough to keep your pony in your backyard.

British stables

Typically in the U.K., each stall opens onto a central courtyard called the yard, which lets the horses see what is going on. An overhanging roof gives the horses (and people) some protection from sun and rain.

Planning a conversion

You may have a garage or outbuilding at home that can be turned into a barn. In most areas your parents will have to apply with local zoning boards for permission to keep "livestock." They will have to submit plans to the board. This process can take a long time.

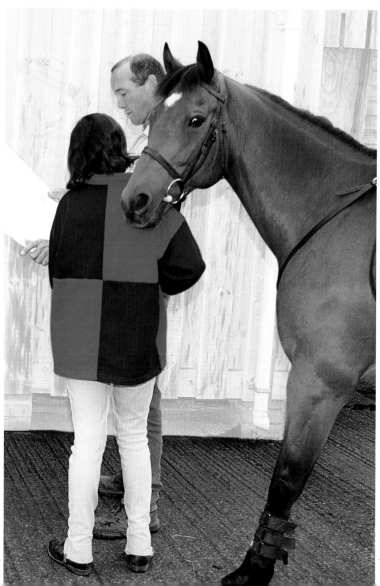

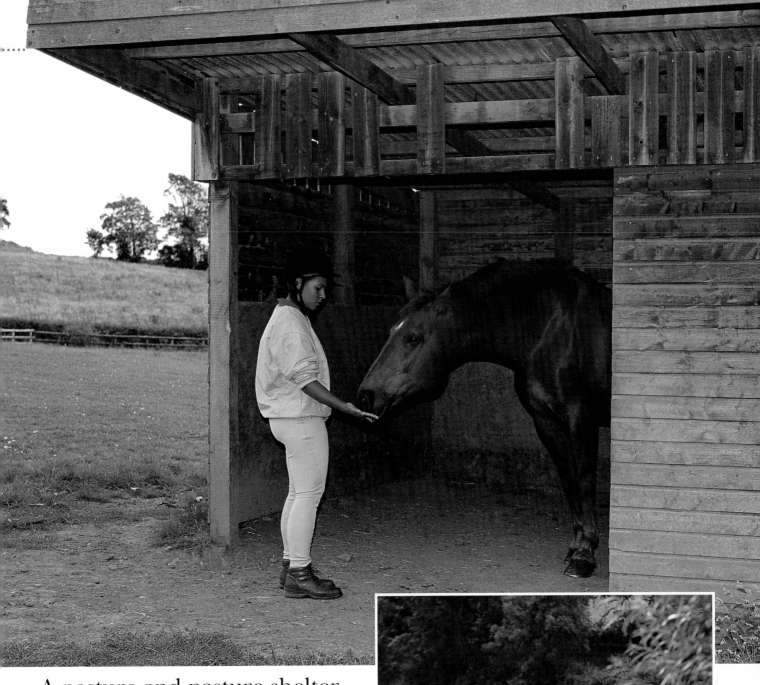

A pasture and pasture shelter

If you only have a pasture in which to keep
your pony, try to make sure there is some kind of
shelter. This will protect your pony from the weather,
as well as giving you a place where you can put your
belongings, groom the pony, tack it up, and feed it in
the winter. Remember not to leave tack in the shelter.

A farmer's pasture

A local farmer may let you rent a pasture and
possibly a stall too, although many do not like
having horses on their land. If you do find one
who is willing, it can be very useful because he
will probably be able to supply you with hay
and may even let you ride in his pasture.

A barn of your own

If you want to keep a pony in your own barn at home, you need to plan well beforehand. The barn does not have to be perfect or even conventional, but it must meet certain basic requirements and be safe and comfortable for the pony.

A converted building

You may be lucky enough to have a building at home that you can use as a stable. It must be in good condition with a weatherproof roof and a safe floor. It must also be well ventilated.

A ready-made stable

You can buy a wooden stable as a kit and have it assembled at your home. You will need some kind of level, solid base on which to stand it. This will probably mean laying a concrete slab. You need to consider the site you will use carefully before you go ahead.

Planning a barn

If you are considering keeping a pony at home, remember you will need more than just a building in which to house it. Although you may only be planning to use one stall, you will have to find space for storing feed, hay, and bedding, and the latter two take up a lot of room. You must reserve a corner not too near the building for the manure pile. Tack and blankets have to be kept somewhere, and if you do not have a paddock, you will have to find a pasture for a daily turnout.

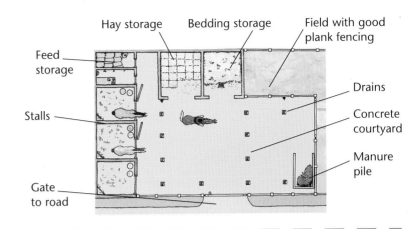

Feed storage
Hay storage
Bedding storage
Field with good plank fencing
Stalls
Gate to road
Drains
Concrete courtyard
Manure pile

A stable's requirements

When you are planning your stable, you need to make sure you have enough space. The stall has to be large enough—about 12 x 12 feet for a pony. The doorway and ceiling must be high enough for it not to bang its head if it tosses it up in the air. You will need a water supply nearby. Electricity is useful, but not absolutely essential. If you do have it, you must install light bulbs and switches where the pony cannot reach them.

Tying ring
It is useful to have tying rings both inside and outside the stall for tying up the pony and for hanging a haynet.

Dutch doors
The open top half of the door allows the pony to look out. It should always be left open for ventilation.

Automatic waterer
This needs to be plumbed in, but it will save a lot of time and effort carrying water buckets.

Louvered windows
The top half of the windows should open inward to let in air but not rain, and the glass should be protected by grillwork.

Manger
A pony or horse can drink and eat from a bowl or bucket put on the floor, but a manger is less likely to become dirty.

Door bolts
Some ponies can undo the top bolts on their doors. A bolt with a lockable end prevents them from doing this.

Good drainage
A concrete or brick floor that slopes gently to a drain will provide good stable drainage. A dirt floor can also be used.

Kick bolt
A foot-operated kick bolt on the lower part of the door saves having to bend down—which is useful when carrying things.

Wheelbarrow   Shovel

Four-pronged
pitchfork

Broom

Shavings
pitchfork

Mucking out equipment

To muck out a stall you need a pitchfork and a shovel for removing droppings and wet bedding, a broom for sweeping the stall and barn, and a wheelbarrow to carry the muck to the manure pile.

Stable management

Stable management means the organization and carrying out of all the tasks that are centered around the stable. A large part of stable management is the daily routine of mucking out, feeding, and watering, as well as keeping the building and its areas clean. Other jobs include the maintenance of equipment and checking feed and bedding storage areas.

Mucking out

A stall needs a thorough mucking out once a day— removing the droppings and wet bedding—and skipping out—just removing the droppings—several times a day. The process is much the same for straw or shavings. Some people use a deep litter system, in which only the droppings are removed daily and fresh bedding is added.

Clearing up
Sweep any remaining manure and wet bedding into a pile in the middle of the floor and use the shovel to put it all into the wheelbarrow. Continue sweeping until the floor is clean.

1 First remove all the obvious droppings on the surface with the shavings pitchfork and put them in the wheelbarrow.

2 When you have done this, toss the shavings to the sides of the stall, removing any droppings that fall out of them as you do so.

3 Once you have removed the top shavings, those still on the floor will be wet. Scoop them up with the shavings pitchfork.

4 Now the dry bedding is stacked around the sides and wet shavings have been removed. You can sweep the floor and shovel up the manure.

Bedding storage

Shavings and straw bales must be stored somewhere. Straw must be stacked under cover, preferably in a hay barn, where air can circulate around it and prevent it from becoming dusty or moldy. Shavings can be stacked outside, preferably under a waterproof cover.

Clean water

Horses and ponies should have access to clean water at all times. Whenever you visit the stall, check the bucket to see if it needs more water. If the water is dirty, throw it away and rinse the bucket out well before refilling it. Every few days, scrub out the water bucket to keep it clean.

Water buckets are usually made of plastic or rubber.

A neat manure pile

Try to keep the manure pile neat. Ideally you should divide it into three sections: one that you are using to tip the manure on each day, one that you are leaving to rot down, and one that has already rotted down to be used as compost or disposed of elsewhere.

5 If possible, leave the floor to dry and air for a while before pulling back the shavings to lay the bed. Bank up the shavings against the walls.

6 You may not always need to add new shavings, but when you do, open the bale carefully, cutting the tape with scissors or a special safety barn knife that has a recessed blade.

7 Shavings are very tightly packed in their bales. It is often easiest to use the four-pronged pitchfork to loosen them if you do not need to add a whole new bale to the bedding.

Choosing a pasture

A pasture suitable for grazing by horses and ponies should be level and well drained. It needs some form of shade and shelter (for example, trees, hedges, or a pasture shelter), secure and safe fencing, a clean water supply, safe access from the road, and a safely hung gate that can be locked if necessary. The pasture and hedges should not contain any poisonous plants.

Good fencing

Plank fencing is the best kind of fencing for horses and ponies, but some people use wooden post and rail *(above)*. Electric fencing works well if you keep it off the ground and check the supply regularly.

Good grazing

Horses and ponies thrive on a mixture of grasses, such as rye, timothy, and meadow fescue, with some beneficial herbs and weeds, such as dandelion, chicory, and yarrow. Be careful— do not let a hay-fed horse graze for long periods. Rich grasses may make it sick.

Poisonous plants

You should check any pasture in which you are going to keep a pony for poisonous plants. Any you find should be dug up and burned. If the pasture is near a garden, check that the pony cannot reach plants such as rhododendron, laburnum, oleander, and evergreen hedges. Most evergreens are poisonous.

Foxglove

Deadly nightshade

Ragwort

Hemlock

Horsetail

Signs of a bad pasture

A pasture that is covered in droppings and has more weeds than grass, broken fencing, and a gate held in place with string is not suitable for a pony.

Uneven grazing
Clumps of coarse grass surrounded by bare pasture usually mean that the pasture has been overgrazed. It needs to be mowed and rested before being used again for horses or ponies.

Water supply

A stream is not ideal because it may be polluted. A water trough that fills automatically is very useful, or you may have to use buckets. Both the trough and the buckets need a good scrubbing regularly to remove the algae that builds up.

Muddy pasture
A poorly-drained pasture with too many animals on it in the winter can quickly become badly cut up and muddy and is no use for grazing.

Secure locks
Unless the pasture is well supervised, keep the gate locked as a precaution against theft.

Too many droppings
A pasture covered in piles of droppings needs to be cleared and rested. The droppings kill the grass and contain many worm eggs. Grazing around these areas reinfests a horse.

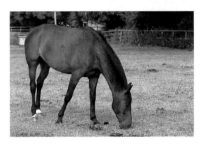

Safe gate

A correctly-hung and well-maintained gate that does not sag on its hinges, drag on the ground as you open and close it, or swing back and hit you as you go through ensures you can lead your pony into the pasture safely. The gate may be made of wood or metal.

Barbwire fencing
Barbwire should **never** be used for fencing where horses and ponies are kept. Many have been injured by it. The wire is especially dangerous if it is rusty or sagging.

Rhododendron

Laburnum

Yew

Bracken

Oak (acorns)

Laurel

Caring for a pasture

A pony's pasture needs a lot of attention to stay in good condition. Horses and ponies tend to graze in parts of a pasture until they are bare, leaving patches of coarse grass and weeds untouched. Putting other animals in the pasture evens out the grazing, but it may also need to be spread with fertilizer or lime and rolled in the spring if it gets churned up in the winter.

Pulling up ragwort

Ragwort is a tall, poisonous plant with small, yellow, daisylike flowers and ragged leaves. You should check a pony's paddock regularly for ragwort and pull or dig up any immediately. All traces of the plant should be destroyed. Put salt in the hole left after pulling it up to kill any remaining roots.

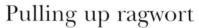

Removing droppings

Leaving droppings around not only damages the grass, but also encourages parasitic worms to breed. In a small pasture you should remove droppings every day with a shovel and a wheelbarrow or skip. This may not be practical if horses or ponies graze a large pasture, so the area should be dragged or harrowed instead to break up and scatter the droppings. The sun will then dry them out and kill off any worm eggs.

Pasture rotation

Grazing a pony paddock with sheep or cattle is one way to stop worm eggs developing because the worms can live only in horses' and ponies' digestive systems. If possible, a pasture should be grazed in rotation by horses, cattle, and sheep.

Mowing a pasture

Once or twice each summer a pasture needs to be mowed. A tractor pulls a machine that cuts down weeds, such as docks, nettles, and thistles, as well as the long, coarse grasses. This helps to stunt the weeds' growth and prevents them from scattering seeds. It also encourages new grass shoots to flourish, which provide more nourishing grazing.

Removing stones

Small stones can get lodged in a horse's or pony's hooves and cause lameness. Large stones can be dangerous if horses or ponies gallop around a pasture, causing them to stumble, sprain tendons, or even fall. It is a good idea to remove as many stones from your pony's pasture as you can.

Clearing trash

If a pasture is near a road, litter such as string (*left*) and plastic (*right*) may blow or be thrown into it. Plastic bags can kill a pony if eaten, and cans and glass bottles can cause severe cuts. String can become entangled around a horse's legs and also causes problems if eaten. You should check a pasture daily and remove any litter you find.

Turning out and catching

Turning out means putting a horse or pony out in a pasture. It is better to remove its halter to avoid any possibility of it getting tangled on fences or hedges, but leather halters, which break when caught on something, can be left on ponies that are difficult to catch. If your pony gets excited at the thought of joining its friends in the pasture, try to keep it calm.

Turning out a horse or pony

As you lead your pony toward the pasture other horses or ponies already there may gather around the gate. If this happens, ask a helper to open the gate for you and shoo the horses away quietly so that you can take the pony into the pasture safely.

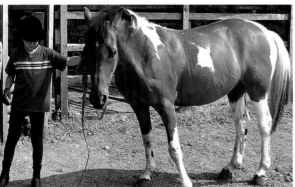

1 Lead the pony a few yards into the pasture after closing the gate behind you. Turn it around to face the gate, and undo the buckle on the halter.

2 Slip the halter off its head gently, and let it walk quietly away. If it gets excited and tries to whip around and gallop off, make sure you keep out of its way.

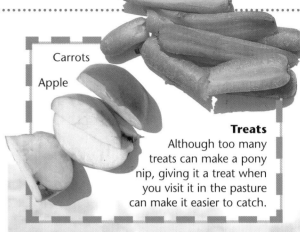

Carrots

Apple

Treats
Although too many treats can make a pony nip, giving it a treat when you visit it in the pasture can make it easier to catch.

Leading a pony

Ponies are usually led on the left-hand side. Hold the rope so that your right hand is near the pony's head with the palm facing down, and your left hand is near the end of the rope. Look straight ahead and walk level with the pony's shoulder.

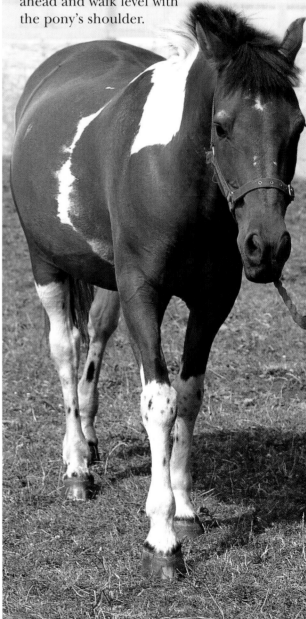

Keeping hold of a pony

If the pony misbehaves, bring your right hand down to the end of the rope near your left hand. Try your best not to let go, but bring the pony around you in a circle. Never wrap the rope around your hands. If the pony pulls away, it will drag you along.

Catching a horse or pony

Some horses and ponies are easier to catch than others. Approach a difficult horse with the halter behind your back and your hand outstretched holding a treat or a bucket with some feed in it. If the pony runs away, do not chase it. Wait for it to come to you.

1 Walk toward the horse's shoulder from the front, holding out a treat in your hand so that it can see it.

2 Give the pony the treat and quickly slip the lead rope around its neck before the pony has time to move away.

3 Put the halter over the horse's nose, still keeping the rope around its neck in case it decides to wander off.

4 Reach under its jaw with your right hand, and grab hold of the headpiece. Pass it over the top of the horse's head. Grab hold of the halter's cheekpiece with your other hand.

5 Buckle the headpiece so that it fits correctly—not too tight or too loose (page 42). Tuck the end of the strap through the buckle to keep it out of the way. You can then lead the horse in from the pasture.

Feeding a pony

A pony's natural food is grass. It has to eat a lot, but only a little at a time, to provide nourishment. When we replace grass with hay and other food, we must stick to this natural eating routine.

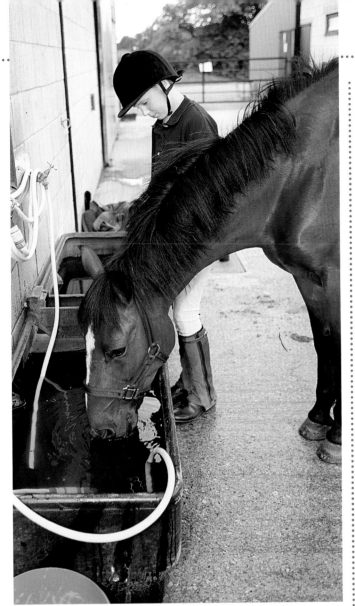

Plenty of clean water

Clean water should always be available to a horse or pony. If it is not possible to allow it free access to water, then offer water at regular intervals before feeding. Watering after feeding can cause digestive problems, such as colic.

The rules of feeding

Horses' and ponies' stomachs are small, and their intestines are large. They need small quantities of food at a time, but a lot overall. This is how they eat bulk food such as grass or hay. But with concentrated feed (pages 24–25), it is important that they do not get too much food in their stomachs at once.

Feeding rules

Feed little and often, rather than giving large feeds.

Only feed fresh food.

Match the amount of food to the work the pony does.

Do not exercise a pony immediately after feeding.

Introduce new foods gradually to a pony's diet.

Feed plenty of bulk food, such as good grass hay.

Allow the pony to graze in a pasture for part of each day.

Feed a stabled pony something succulent, such as carrots or apples.

Feed at regular times each day of the week.

Keep the manger clean.

A haynet keeps hay off the floor.

Regular feeds

It is best to give a pony concentrated feed rations in several small feeds evenly spaced during the day. Work out a routine that you can manage, and stick to it. Ponies do not understand the difference between a weekday and a weekend— they expect their food to appear at the same time every day.

Different kinds of feed

H orse and pony feed can be divided into two main types. Bulk feed—grass and hay—forms the major part of the diet. A pony may manage on that alone. If it works hard, it may need up to 30 percent of its rations in the form of concentrated feed—also called hard feed.

Tying a quick-release knot

Make a loop in the rope and pull it through the tying ring. Twist the base of the loop several times.

Make a second loop in the loose end of the rope, and then push this through the first loop you have made.

Tighten the knot by pulling on the attached end of the rope. Undo the knot by pulling on the loose end.

Filling a haynet

Feeding hay on the floor is wasteful because the hay gets trampled and dirty. To fill a haynet, open it as wide as possible. Tear a slice of hay off the bale, pull it apart, and push it into the center of the haynet. You can get a rough idea of how much you are feeding by counting the number of slices you put in each time.

How much hay?
To be sure exactly how much you are feeding, weigh the filled haynet.

Hanging a haynet

The haynet should be tied up high to prevent the horse from pawing at it and getting its foot stuck in it. Using a quick-release knot makes it easy to undo when it is empty.

1 Put the string of the haynet through the tying ring in the stall. Pull on the string to raise the haynet to the right height.

2 Loop the string through the rope mesh near the bottom of the haynet, and take it back up to the tying ring.

3 Put the end of the string through the tying ring again and tie the haynet firmly with a quick-release knot.

Types of concentrated feed

Oats can make ponies unmanageable so it may be better to feed barley instead. Most concentrated feed is best mixed with chopped hay and straw. Bran is used in mashes. Corn should be fed sparingly; sugar beet must be soaked in water before feeding. Pellets and sweet feed are easy to feed.

Pellets

Sweet feed

Flaked corn

Bran

Micronized flaked barley

Pulp

Sugar beet soaked in water

Chopped hay

Crimped oats

How to store feed

Feed must be kept in a cool, dry place and protected from rats and mice. In large stables sacks of concentrated feed are emptied into metal feed containers, but for one pony plastic garbage cans make good substitutes. Hay must be kept in a dry barn where air can circulate around it.

Supplements and treats

All horses and ponies need salt, which can be provided by a mineral block. In the winter feeding a little cod liver oil supplies essential vitamins. Ponies appreciate carrots both as treats and as winter feed. Apples are always very popular, but feeding too many can cause colic.

Mineral block
Ponies enjoy licking and gnawing at mineral blocks both out in the pasture and in their stalls.

Vegetable oils
Ponies need some fat in their diet, and this can be provided by oils such as vegetable oil. About one tablespoonful can be added to a feed.

A diet for your pony

Horses and ponies may be "good doers" or "bad doers." This means they can do well or even get fat on little food, or stay thin while eating a lot. An experienced horseperson will be able to work out a diet for a difficult horse or pony. With most ponies, it is better to be cautious about feeding, and if in doubt, give less rather than more. It is not healthy for a pony to be overweight.

Working out your pony's weight

You can check your pony's weight with a weight tape—a kind of tape measure. You pass the weight tape around the pony's girth, and as well as reading the measurement, you can also read off its weight. You may need an assistant on the other side of the pony to check that the tape is in the right position. You can also weigh the pony on a weighbridge.

Too thin or too fat?

Although they may both be the same height, a stockily built pony, such as a Highland, will carry much more weight than a thoroughbred type. So you have to assess a pony's fatness according to its type. It is important for the pony's health that it should be the right weight. A thin pony feels the cold. It uses its feed to keep warm, and it may have little energy left for working. A fat pony puts a strain on its joints and heart.

A thin pony
If you can see a pony's ribs, if its hip bones stick out, and its head looks too big for its neck, it is too thin. This may be the result of teeth problems, worms, or lack of food.

A fat pony
When you cannot feel a pony's ribs or spine, and it has thick pads of fat over its shoulders, and a large, round belly, it is too fat. Fat ponies are prone to illnesses such as laminitis (founder).

The perfect weight
A pony's outline should be smooth and rounded without any obvious fat. You should not be able to see its bones, but you should be able to feel them if you prod with a finger.

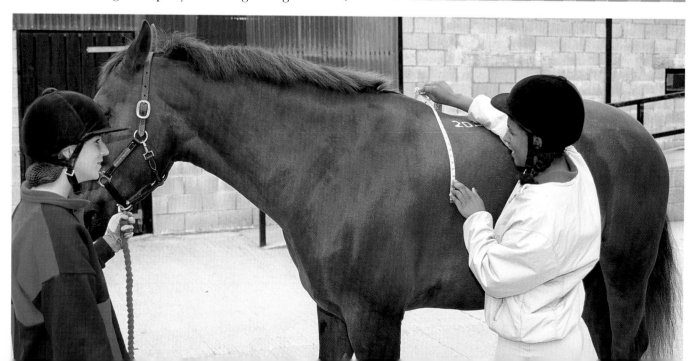

Measuring out

The only way you can be sure how much food your pony is eating is to measure it out. Work out how much food is needed by multiplying the pony's weight by 2.5 and dividing the result by 200. Decide how much of this should be concentrated feed and measure it out for each feed.

Starvation paddock

Lush summer grazing can be too rich for some ponies that become overweight and risk getting laminitis. Although it may sound cruel, they are best kept in an almost bare paddock, where they have to work hard to get grass to eat. An alternative is to stable them for most of the time and only let them out to graze for short periods.

Using a bucket muzzle

This is another way of stopping grazing ponies from eating too much. The muzzle has large holes at the front for breathing and small holes underneath that allow a certain amount of grazing and let the pony drink. The muzzle is held in place by a head strap, which you thread through the rings on the halter.

Soaking a haynet

Ponies that suffer from dust allergies and have breathing difficulties are best fed hay that has been soaked in a tub of water for a short while. A plastic garbage can is ideal. Filled haynets can be very heavy when wet, so be careful not to strain your back when lifting them out.

Weighing hay

It is a good idea to weigh filled haynets so that you know exactly how much hay the pony is being fed. You can buy special spring balances, which you can hang in the feed room or on a gate, designed to weigh a filled haynet. If you are feeding your pony soaked hay, weigh it before you soak it.

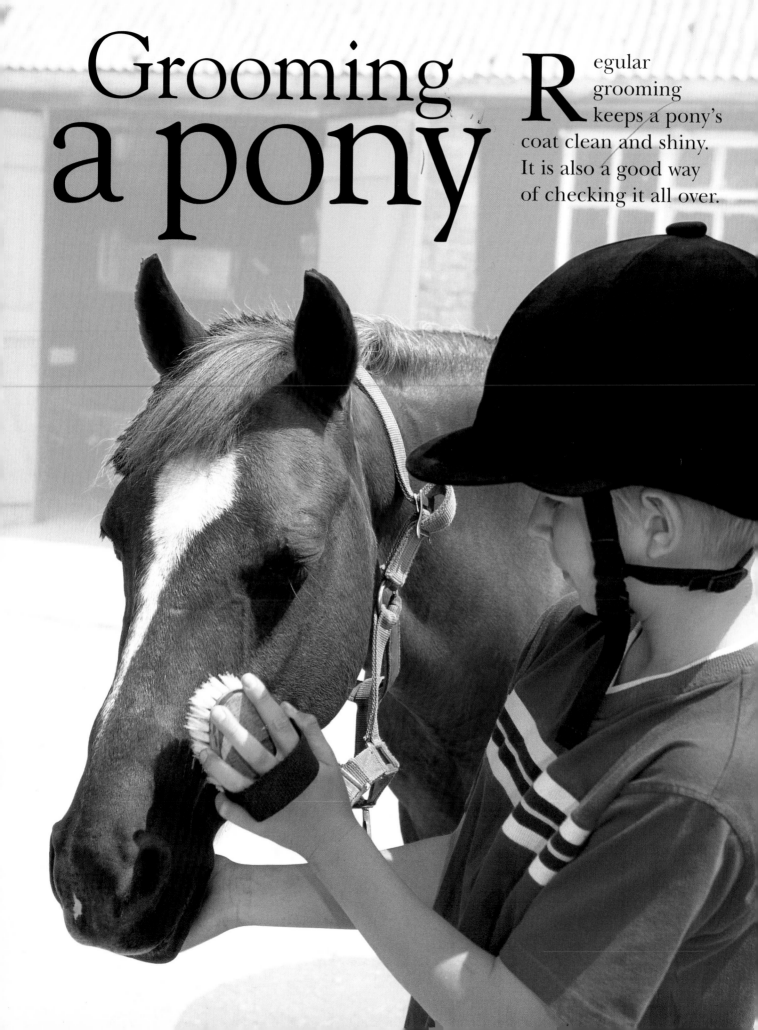

Grooming a pony

R egular grooming keeps a pony's coat clean and shiny. It is also a good way of checking it all over.

Grooming equipment

Grooming means cleaning the pony's coat, combing out its mane and tail, picking out its hooves, and keeping its eyes, nostrils, muzzle, and dock area clean. Each of these tasks needs a particular piece of equipment. Using the right equipment for each part of the grooming process enables you to carry out the work more efficiently.

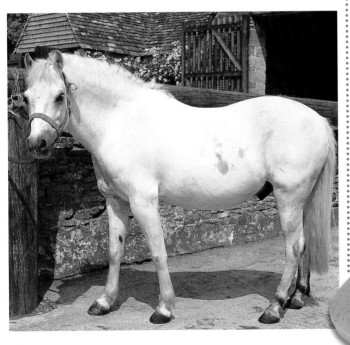

Why do I need to groom?

A healthy, hard-working pony needs grooming every day to keep its skin clean and in good condition. But all ponies need brushing over regularly to remove dried mud and stable stains and to keep the mane and tail neat. This not only makes them look better, but the ponies are also more pleasant to handle, and you and your clothes will stay cleaner.

Parts of the grooming kit

Ideally you need all the different grooming aids shown here, but you could start with a few and build up gradually. To begin with, a dandy brush, body brush, metal curry comb, hoof pick, and sponges are the most important things.

A dandy brush has stiff bristles and is used for removing dried mud.

A body brush has short bristles, designed to remove dirt and loose hair from the pony's coat and skin.

A plastic or rubber curry comb is used to remove mud and loosen matted dirt.

A metal curry comb is pulled across a body brush to clean it. It is not for use on the pony.

A hoof pick, which may have a brush attached, is used to remove dirt and stones from the hooves.

A water brush is used damp to lay the pony's mane and tail in place as a finishing touch.

A mane comb is mostly used when pulling the mane and tail to neaten them and separate the hairs before braiding.

Hoof oil is applied to the hooves with a brush to give a shiny finish for a special occasion.

One sponge is used to clean the eyes, nose, and muzzle; the other to clean the dock area.

A stable rubber or towel is used at the end of the grooming routine to remove any remaining traces of dust.

Grooming routines

A pasture-kept pony should only be brushed over lightly with a dandy brush to keep it neat. A hard-working, stabled pony needs to be groomed thoroughly each day to keep its skin in good condition. Both the dandy and body brushes are used in the direction of the hair of the pony's coat.

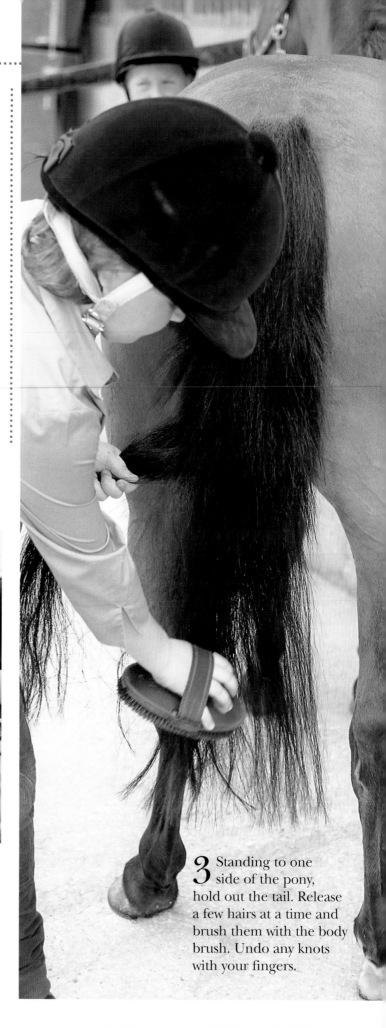

Clean the body brush on the metal curry comb after every three or four strokes.

1 For a thorough grooming, first tie up the pony. Starting at the top of its neck on the left-hand side, groom it all over using the body brush.

2 Then undo the halter and rope. Fasten the halter around its neck while you brush its face gently with the body brush or a special face brush.

3 Standing to one side of the pony, hold out the tail. Release a few hairs at a time and brush them with the body brush. Undo any knots with your fingers.

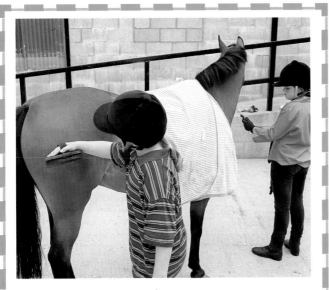

Quartering

Quartering means a quick brushing over of a horse or pony to remove stable stains and shavings or straw from the mane and tail. This will make it look neat before going out for exercise. The real work of grooming is done after exercise. In cold weather the blanket can be left over the forehand or quarters to keep the pony warm.

Fold back the blanket over the pony's quarters while grooming its forehand. Do both sides, then fold the blanket forward over its forehand so you can groom its quarters.

Sponging eyes, nose, and dock

The corners of a pony's eyes, the nostrils, the muzzle, if it is dirty, and the dock area under the tail should be cleaned every day with damp sponges. Use different sponges for the face and for the dock, and remember which is which!

1 Dampen the sponge, squeeze out the water, and wipe the corners of the eyes downward.

2 Rinse the sponge and use it to clean around the pony's mouth and inside its nostrils.

3 Using a different sponge, clean the dock, including the underside of the tail.

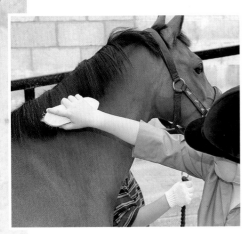

4 To clean the mane and remove any tangles, first brush it out thoroughly with the body brush. For a final, neat finish, dampen the water brush and use it to lay the mane in place.

5 Although dried mud should be removed first, you can use a plastic or rubber curry comb instead of a dandy brush to remove any you may have missed on the legs.

6 The final step is to go all over the pony's body with a stable rubber. This is a cotton cloth that removes any remaining traces of dust and loose hairs and gives a glossy finish to the coat.

Hoof and foot care

Taking care of a horse's or pony's hooves is one of the most important tasks an owner must carry out. A pony's hooves must be sound. You should check and clean out a pony's hooves before and after riding, and on nonriding days, do it at least once. You must also have them regularly trimmed by a farrier and shod (pages 44–45) if you ride on rough tracks and roads.

When feet need attention

If a pony's hooves have not been trimmed regularly, the horn of the hoof will grow long and ragged and may split. When a pony does a lot of road work, the shoes will wear thin quickly and need renewing regularly. Overgrowth of the hooves makes the shoe nails come loose, and the shoe may come off.

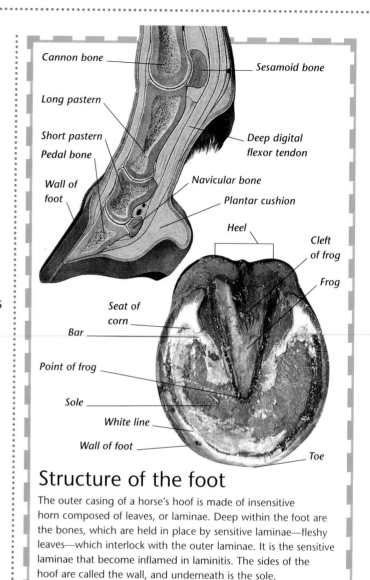

Structure of the foot

The outer casing of a horse's hoof is made of insensitive horn composed of leaves, or laminae. Deep within the foot are the bones, which are held in place by sensitive laminae—fleshy leaves—which interlock with the outer laminae. It is the sensitive laminae that become inflamed in laminitis. The sides of the hoof are called the wall, and underneath is the sole.

Overgrown hooves
If the hoof is allowed to become overgrown, the toes get too long and turn up, and the pony's weight goes back on its heels, altering the foot's balance. It can take a long time to correct this.

Raised clenches
When the hoof has been neglected and allowed to grow too long, the clenches (the ends of the nails that hold the shoe on) rise out of the hoof wall. The pony can injure itself on them and may lose the shoe.

Stones lodged in the hoof

Sometimes horses pick up small stones in their hooves, which lodge in the grooves on either side of the frog. If they get wedged in, they can damage the hoof, causing pain and lameness. You can remove them by digging them out with a hoof pick.

Picking up and cleaning out a hoof

Be positive in your actions when you pick up a pony's foot. Slide your hand firmly down each leg so that you do not tickle it. Always use a hoof pick from the heel of the foot to the toe, paying particular attention to the grooves between the frog and the bars and to the cleft of the frog itself.

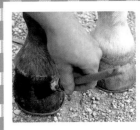

Oiling the hooves

Applying hoof oil to a horse's hooves makes them look shiny, but you should not do it too often or it can prevent the hoof from absorbing moisture. Pick out the hooves and scrub off any mud with a water brush before you start. Let the hooves dry, then apply the oil with a small brush. Hoof oil will not improve the quality of the hoof's horn. Only a special diet can do this.

1 When you want to pick up and examine a pony's hind hoof, start by putting your hand on the side of its hindquarters and sliding it down toward its leg.

2 Pass your hand firmly down the back of its hind leg. Do not be nervous when you are handling a pony or it will sense it and become nervous as well.

3 Continue down the back of its leg until you reach the hock. Keep your own feet away from the pony's in case it treads on you.

4 When you reach the pony's hock, bring your hand around to the front of its leg and move down over the cannon bone.

5 When you reach the fetlock joint, grasp it firmly and try to lift it, saying "Up" as you do so. Crouch—do not kneel—beside the pony.

6 Hold the pony's hoof in one hand while you use the hoof pick from the heel toward the toe in the other. A skip is useful for the dirt.

Washing a pony

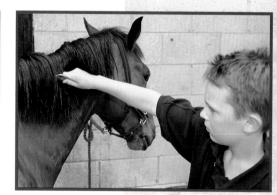

O nly wash a horse or pony if it is absolutely necessary. Choose a warm, sunny, and windless day. Washing removes much of the oil from a horse's or pony's coat. This makes them look clean and shiny, but means that until the oil builds up again, they will feel the cold and have no protection against the rain. They may need to wear a blanket if the weather turns cooler.

Bucket of water

Shampoo

Sweat scraper   Sponge

Equipment for washing
Before you start collect all the necessary equipment and put it where you can easily reach it.

Washing routine

It is important to keep the shampoo out of the pony's eyes, so when you are washing its neck and mane make sure its head is held up. Do not shampoo its face, just wipe it over with a clean, damp sponge.

1 Tie up the pony where the water can drain away. Fill a bucket with warm water and mix in the shampoo.

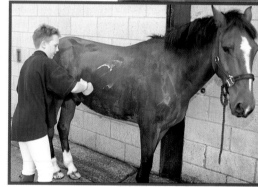

2 Dip the sponge in the water and rub it over the pony's coat in the direction of the hair. Cover the whole body, but not the head.

3 Wash the mane with the sponge, then rinse off all traces of the shampoo with another sponge and several buckets of water, or use a hose if the pony does not mind.

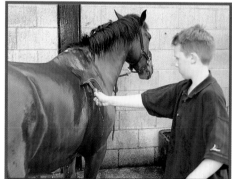

4 After rinsing use the sweat scraper to remove the excess water, pulling it across the pony's body following the lie of the coat. If you do not have a sweat scraper, you can use the side of your hand.

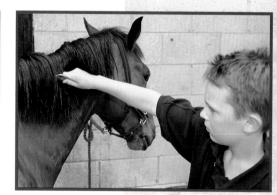

5 Gently comb out the wet mane. If there are knots and tangles in it, undo them carefully with your fingers before combing. Do not try to drag them out with the comb or you will pull out the hairs.

Rinsing the saddle patch

In warm weather when a horse returns from exercise with a sweaty saddle patch, you can hose it down—if this does not scare it—or sponge off the sweat.

1 Wash the top of the tail with a wet sponge, warm water, and shampoo, as you did the pony's body.

2 Rinse the tail in several buckets of clean water, swishing it around with your hand.

Washing a pony's tail

A pony's tail may need washing frequently, especially if it is a pale color. Doing so will not chill the pony. Use a bucket of warm water and shampoo, lifting up the bucket to get as much of the tail in it as possible. Hold up the bucket with one hand while you squeeze dirt out of the tail with the other.

6 Rub an old towel all over the pony in the direction of the hair to dry it off as much as possible. Squeeze out the water from its mane in the towel, and dry its neck underneath it. Do not forget to dry the pony's legs and heels as well.

7 On a hot day the pony will dry off naturally in the sun. If the sky clouds over, put an antisweat sheet or a cooler blanket over it, and walk the pony around until it is dry to prevent it from catching a chill.

Clipping a pony

Horses and ponies grow thick coats in the winter. If they are worked hard, they sweat a lot and become fatigued. To avoid this, the areas where they sweat the most have the hair clipped off. A clipped horse or pony needs a blanket to keep it warm when it is not working, even if it lives in a stable. Clippers must be handled with care, and the job is best done by an adult.

The hair is completely clipped off from the horse's head and neck.

Bandit clip
The horse is clipped all over except for its face, where the hair is left as protection from the rain. It is also a useful clip for a head-shy horse.

A bib clip runs in a straight line down the side of the neck.

Bib clip
The pony is clipped on the face and the front of the neck, chest, and shoulders. This clip is used for a horse or pony that sweats a lot on the neck.

Hunter clip
All the hair is clipped except for the saddle patch and the legs, which are left unclipped for protection against sores and thorns.

Belly clip
The hair is removed from the belly and up between the forelegs. A variation is to clip the hair on the underside of the neck too.

Different types of clips

The different styles of clips reflect the amount of work a horse or pony is expected to do. Some hard-working horses are fully clipped; others have areas of winter coat left on for protection against the weather, saddle sores, cuts, and thorns.

Trace clip
This is a popular clip for working ponies. Hair is removed from the underside of the neck, the belly, and the lower part of the body.

Clipping equipment

Clipping machines are usually electrically operated. They have a number of blades, from fine to coarse, depending on the type of hair to be cut. The blades need oiling and cleaning regularly when in use.

Main clippers

Small clippers

The blanket area keeps the horse warm and dry.

The coat is cut in a semicircle where the flank joins the quarters, following the line of the hair.

The clipping line at the top of the legs always slopes down from front to back.

The clippers are used with even pressure against the lie of the coat. They should move parallel to the skin without digging into it.

Blades for trimming coarse hair

Brush for cleaning clippers

Blades for trimming fine hair

Oils to lubricate clippers

CLIPPER OIL

Blanket clip

This clip gets its name from the blanket area left unclipped on the back, which protects fine-coated horses against bad weather. The legs are also left unclipped. It is a useful clip for hard-working horses and is often used as an alternative to the hunter clip. With this clip, as with others, the areas to be left are marked out in chalk before clipping.

Using the clippers

Clippers should always be used with a circuit-breaker to cut off the electricity if anything goes wrong. It is a good idea to wear rubber-soled shoes. The horse's coat must be clean and dry, and a haynet may help keep it quiet.

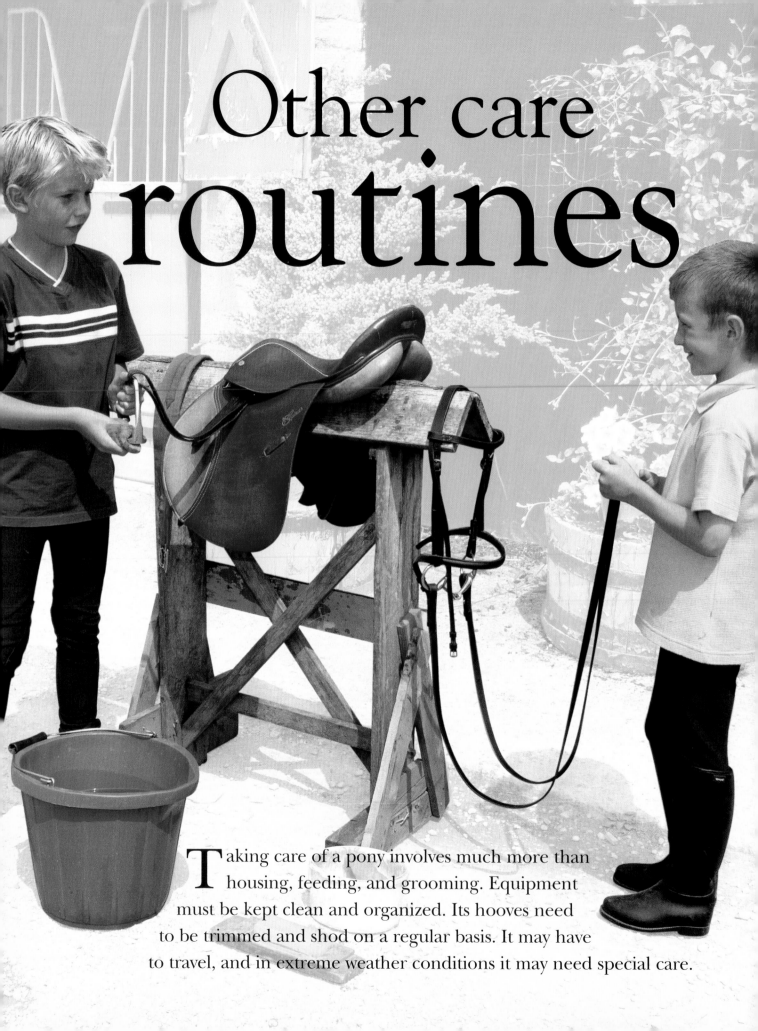

Other care
routines

Taking care of a pony involves much more than housing, feeding, and grooming. Equipment must be kept clean and organized. Its hooves need to be trimmed and shod on a regular basis. It may have to travel, and in extreme weather conditions it may need special care.

Checking the legs
When you get back to the stable, check the pony's legs for small cuts or any thorns it may have picked up, and feel for any heat or swelling.

Walking home
When you are not on a busy road, loosen the girth by one hole, and let your pony walk on a loose rein to stretch its neck muscles.

At the end of a ride

Horses and ponies can get hot, sweaty, and excitable during a ride. Always walk your pony the last mile or two home to let it cool off and calm down. At the end of a hard day, dismount, run the stirrups up, loosen the girth, and lead it home.

Rubbing the ears
A tired, wet horse may have cold ears. You can restore the circulation to the ears by grasping them at the base and pulling them gently through your cupped hands.

All blanketed up
If the pony is dry, brush off any mud before putting on its blanket. If it is wet, put straw under the blanket. Bandage wet and muddy legs over straw or cotton padding.

Care after exercise

On your return home unsaddle the pony, check it over, and clean its hooves. Brush off any mud or sweat marks. In hot weather you can sponge these off. Put on its blanket or an antisweat sheet, and if it is tired and thirsty, offer it half a bucket of lukewarm water. You can give it more later. Give a stabled pony a haynet before its feed. If it is pasture kept and it is not cold or sweating, you can turn it out.

Choosing a blanket

When a horse or pony has been clipped, it needs to wear a blanket to make up for the loss of its winter coat and to keep it warm. On cold winter nights it may need more than one blanket or an extra sheet under the blanket. To be comfortable, the blanket should be long enough to cover the belly and should reach down to the root of the tail. Clipped horses are turned out in a turnout blanket to keep off the rain.

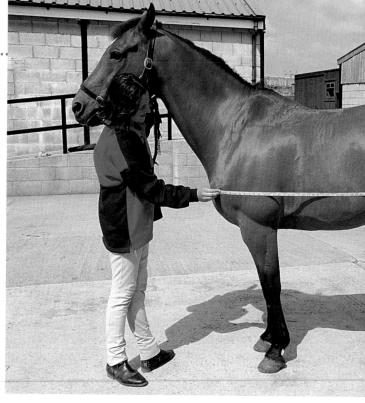

Measuring for a blanket

You need a long tape measure and an assistant to do this. Measure from the center of the horse's chest to the farthest point of its hindquarters. Blanket sizes go up in about 3 inch increments, so you have to buy the nearest size.

Types of blankets

Blankets are made in a variety of styles, shapes, and materials. The latter may be natural, such as cotton, wool, or canvas; or synthetic, usually nylon or polyester. All blankets fasten across the front of the chest with either one or two straps. They are then held in place either by a roller, which goes across the horse's back and around its belly like a girth, or by crossed surcingles. These are sewn onto the right-hand side of the blanket and pass under the horse's belly to fasten on the left side, crossing over from front to back. There are special kinds of blankets for specific purposes, although most horses and ponies just need a stable blanket and a New Zealand rug.

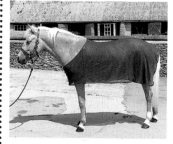

An antisweat sheet is a mesh blanket used on a sweating horse to prevent chills as it cools down.

A stable blanket keeps the horse warm indoors. It may be quilted or made of canvas.

A New Zealand rug is waterproof. It is used when the horse is out in the pasture in the winter.

A summer sheet is a cotton blanket used to keep the horse clean at shows and when traveling.

An exercise sheet is used to keep the horse's back warm during winter exercise.

A hooded New Zealand rug also keeps the pony's neck warm in bad winter weather.

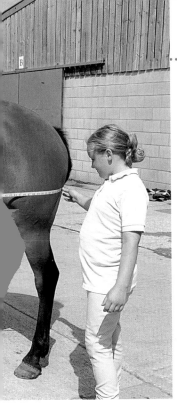

How to put on a blanket

When you put on a pony's blanket, do not fling it onto the pony's back—lower it gently. Put the blanket on forward of where it should lie, so you can slide it back into place, leaving the pony's coat lying flat.

Crossed surcingles

These should be adjusted by sliding the buckles so they fit comfortably around the pony's belly. They do not need to be tight—there should be room for your hand to fit between them and the pony.

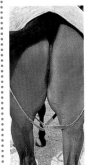

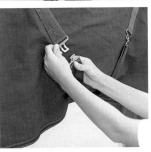

1 Tie up the pony. Carry the blanket folded in half with the back part folded forward over the front part.

2 Holding the blanket in both hands, lower it carefully onto the pony's back in front of where it should fit.

3 Unfold the back part of the blanket and lay it over the pony's quarters. Check that it is lying straight.

4 Fasten the breast straps, and then slide the blanket back until it lies in the correct position on the pony's back.

5 Undo the surcingles on the right side. Reach under the pony's belly for them from the left and fasten them.

6 Finally make sure that the blanket does not press down on the pony's withers and that it is not too tight across the pony's chest.

Roller

A blanket may be held in place with a roller, which fits tightly around the horse. An anticast roller has an arch in the center to prevent a horse from getting stuck, or cast, when it rolls.

Anticast roller

Leg straps

New Zealand rugs are held in place by leg straps, with one looped through the other to prevent them from rubbing. They must be attached correctly.

Taking off a blanket

Tie up the pony. If the blanket has a roller, undo it first and lift it off the pony's back. Make sure that the breast straps, surcingles, and any leg straps are unfastened before removing the rug.

1 When you have undone the surcingles, tie them loosely in place on the right-hand side.

2 Undo the breast straps. Fold the front of the blanket to lie over the back.

3 Holding the folded blanket with both hands, slide it back off the pony's quarters.

A pony's halter

Halters are made either of leather or nylon. They are used to lead a horse or pony and to tie it up. Like bridles, they are made in three basic sizes—pony, cob, and full-size. A very small pony may need a foal halter, which has a number of adjustable straps.

A good fit
This leather halter fits well. It fastens on the pony's left side, and the lead rope is clipped to the round ring under its chin.

Too small
This halter was made to fit a much smaller pony. The headpiece does not even reach far enough to meet the buckle on the cheekpiece.

Too large
This halter is much too large. The pony could pull its head back through it and escape, or get a foot caught in it when grazing or scratching.

Checking the size

A halter needs to fit correctly in the same way as a bridle does. There should be room for you to insert two fingers under the noseband and a hand under the throatlash. A halter that is too tight, especially if it is made of nylon, will rub and may cause sores over the pony's prominent nasal bones.

Fitting and caring for tack

Tack is a horse's or pony's saddle, bridle, halter, and any other saddlery it may wear, such as a martingale. In order for the tack to work correctly, it must fit well, be correctly adjusted, and be well cared for. Neglected tack is dangerous. It can give the pony sores and may break, leading to accidents.

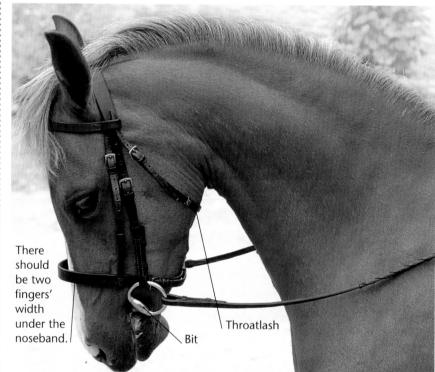

There should be two fingers' width under the noseband.

Bit

Throatlash

Well-fitting bridle

This pony is wearing a well-fitting snaffle bridle with an eggbutt snaffle bit. The browband is at the correct height so it does not pinch the pony's ears, the noseband and throatlash fit well, and the bit just wrinkles the corners of the pony's mouth.

Storing tack

Tack should be cleaned before it is put away. Bridles are hung on arched racks that do not bend the headpieces; saddles are supported on brackets attached to the wall or on free-standing saddle horses.

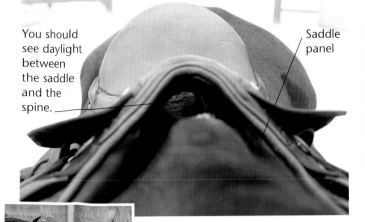

You should see daylight between the saddle and the spine.

Saddle panel

Fitting a saddle

Horses and ponies vary a lot in shape and size, and it is important that the saddle fits well. It must be the right width, and the panel stuffing must be even so the leather maintains a level contact with the pony's back. The saddle must not press on the pony's spine or the withers.

Tacking up

Check that the saddle pad does not press down on the pony's withers. You should be able to insert three fingers between the withers and the pommel of the saddle and two between the girth and the pony.

How to clean tack

It is important to keep saddle and bridle leather clean and supple. If you do so, it will last for many years. You should clean it each time you use it. To clean tack, you need a bucket of warm water, one sponge for cleaning off the dirt and oil, one sponge for saddle-soaping, and a bar of saddle soap.

Wash the bit in clean water and dry it. Clean all the oil and mud off of the bridle with a slightly damp sponge. Then dip the bar of saddle soap into the water and rub it onto your other sponge.

Rub saddle soap well into the leather, undoing fasteners so no parts of the bridle are neglected. Keep moistening the soap when you need more on the sponge. When you have finished, refasten all the buckles.

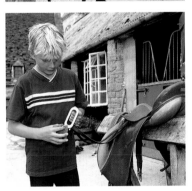

Wipe any mud off the stirrup irons with your cleaning sponge. Rinse the sponge, squeeze it as dry as possible, and clean the oil off of the underside of the saddle, as well as any mud. Do not get the leather too wet.

If you wet the sponge when you are using saddle soap, you will have too much lather. Moisten the soap instead. Rub the sponge all over the saddle. Don't forget the girth billets and stirrup leathers.

Shoeing a pony

Ponies' and horses' hooves grow like your fingernails and need trimming every six to eight weeks to keep them in good condition. Shoeing prevents the hooves from wearing down too quickly when the pony is exercised on hard surfaces like roads. The person who trims and shoes a pony is called a farrier, or blacksmith. Most farriers have mobile forges and travel around to work at their clients' premises.

Hot shoeing

When a shoe is heated in a furnace before being tried on a pony's hoof, the process is called hot shoeing. Because the horn of the foot is insensitive, like your nails, the pony cannot feel it. A pony may need new shoes each time the farrier visits, but if the shoes are not very worn, the farrier will simply reshape them and use them again.

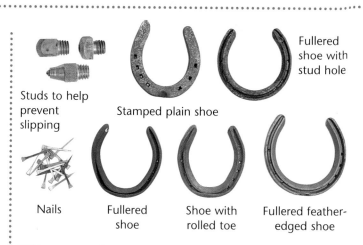

Studs to help prevent slipping

Stamped plain shoe

Fullered shoe with stud hole

Nails

Fullered shoe

Shoe with rolled toe

Fullered feather-edged shoe

Types of shoes

Most horses and ponies wear fullered shoes, which have a groove running around them for better grip in the mud. Farriers can make special types of shoes to correct most horses' and ponies' foot problems, as well as shoes for various kinds of work.

1 Using the buffer and mallet, the farrier cuts the nail ends, or clenches, that hold the shoe onto the foot.

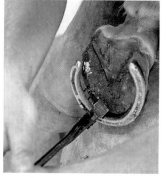

2 When he has cut the clenches, he levers off the shoe with pincers, starting at the heel and moving toward the toe.

3 He neatly cuts away the excess growth of the horn all the way around the hoof using the hoof cutters.

8 He then tries the shoe in place on the hoof. The heat burns the horn, causing it to smoke.

9 When he is satisfied, he cools the shoe in a bucket of water before starting to nail it onto the pony's hoof.

10 He hammers the nails through holes in the shoe to hold it in place, starting at the toe and working back.

Fitting studs

So that horses and ponies can be ridden in wet or muddy conditions, studs are sometimes screwed into special holes in the heels of their shoes.

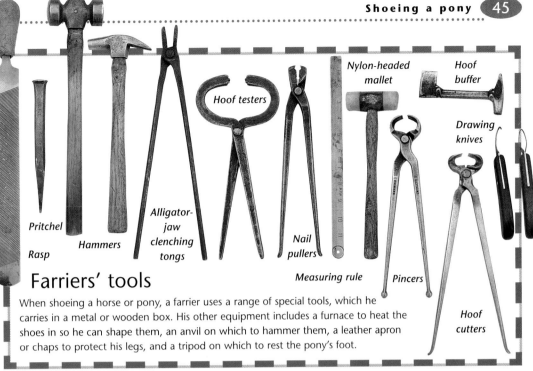

Pritchel

Rasp

Hammers

Alligator-jaw clenching tongs

Hoof testers

Nail pullers

Measuring rule

Nylon-headed mallet

Hoof buffer

Drawing knives

Pincers

Hoof cutters

Farriers' tools

When shoeing a horse or pony, a farrier uses a range of special tools, which he carries in a metal or wooden box. His other equipment includes a furnace to heat the shoes in so he can shape them, an anvil on which to hammer them, a leather apron or chaps to protect his legs, and a tripod on which to rest the pony's foot.

4 He evens out the wall of the hoof, sole, and frog, cutting off any ragged bits with a drawing knife.

5 Using the rasp, he makes sure that the weight-bearing surface of the hoof is absolutely smooth and level.

6 He then heats the shoe in an oven called a furnace until it is red-hot, handling it carefully with pincers.

7 He hammers the hot shoe into shape on the anvil, still holding it with the pincers and reheating it if necessary.

11 The nails come out of the side of the hoof and the farrier twists off their ends with the claw of a hammer.

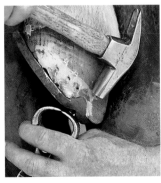

12 Resting the shoe on the pincers, he hammers down the projecting nail ends to form the clenches.

13 With the foot on a tripod, he uses the rasp to smooth the ends of the clenches and the rim of the hoof wall.

14 The finished hoof should look neat and even, with six or more nails holding the new shoe in place.

Traveling safely

If you want to take part in riding club events, shows, or gymkhanas you will need to transport your pony in a van or a trailer. Once they get used to it, most horses and ponies do not mind this and learn to brace themselves against the movement of the vehicle. In doing so, however, they may knock their legs, so they need to wear protective gear. They also wear blankets to keep them warm and clean.

Storage
Water can be carried in a large plastic container.

Providing food and water

While traveling, a haynet will keep your pony happy. Store hay for your return trip inside the trailer rather than hanging it outside where it may be contaminated by exhaust fumes. On a long journey you may also need to take water.

Travel boots
Shaped and padded travel boots fit around the lower part of the pony's legs and are held in place by several Velcro straps.

Boots and bandages

To protect a horse's or pony's legs you can either use special travel boots or bandages. Travel boots cover the legs from the knee or hock to the coronet at the top of the hoof (pages 60–61). If bandages are used, the horse or pony may also need to wear kneecaps and hock boots to cover its joints.

Travel bandages
Used over felt padding, these are put on in the same way as first-aid bandages (pages 54–55).

1 Start by laying the bandage across the top of the pony's tail, leaving the end sticking up.

2 Then take the bandage under the tail and bring it around to the top, holding the end.

3 After a couple of turns of bandage around the tail, fold down the end you left out.

Bandaging a pony's tail

The top part of a pony's tail is bandaged before traveling to stop the pony from rubbing it against the back of the box. Bandaging also lays the hairs flat and keeps the tail neat. The bandage needs to fit firmly. To prevent it from becoming dirty, the bandaged tail can then be folded up and secured with a rubber band.

Travel essentials

Your pony's tack, plus saddle soap, sponges, etc., to give it a final clean up

Your riding clothes if you are going to a show

Food and water —for both you and your pony!

Any documents you may need—tickets, entry forms, etc.

First-aid kit for both of you

Walk confidently up the ramp.

Loading your pony

Most ponies will walk up the ramp of a van or trailer happily, but if yours is unhappy about it, let it take its time. If it still hesitates, ask a helper to put one of the pony's front feet on the ramp. It will then usually walk in without a problem. Food may help.

Don't pull your pony.

Reward your pony when it goes in.

Ready to go

A single pony in a double trailer travels better on the side closer to the center of the road—this trailer *(above)* is in the U.K. In the U.S. a pony on its own should ride on the left. The other side can hold luggage.

Unloading your pony

Untie the pony leaving its rope through the ring so it thinks it is still tied up. If your trailer has a front ramp *(above)*, put it down, remove the tail strap, and lead the pony down the ramp slowly. To unload from the back, ask a helper to stand at the side to keep the pony moving straight back.

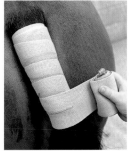

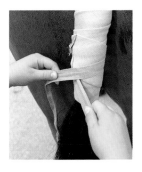

4 Wrap the bandage over the folded-down end to prevent it from slipping.

5 Continue bandaging down the tail until you reach the end of the dock.

6 Cross the strings, take them around to the back, and cross them again.

7 Tie the strings around the bandage in a neat bow to hold it securely in place.

8 Fold a layer of bandage over the bow to stop it from coming undone.

Removing a tail bandage

To remove the tail bandage, unfold the part over the bow, untie the strings, and slide the whole thing off in one movement, laying the hair flat and smooth as you do. Roll up the bandage from the strings' end with the strings folded inside.

Summer and winter care

Extremes of temperature and weather may mean that a horse or pony requires special care. In the hot summer weather horses seek shade and an escape from the flies that can make their lives miserable. In the depths of winter a pasture-kept pony will have little to eat, and the ground may be muddy or frozen. The water supply may freeze up, too. We have to solve all of these problems.

Preventing sunburn

Horses and ponies that have pink noses can suffer from sunburn. It particularly affects stabled animals, who may stand with their heads over the stable door for hours in the sun. You can protect them from sunburn by applying sunblock made for use on human skin.

Fly fringe
A fly fringe can be fitted over a halter or worn on its own. As the horse moves, the strings keep flies out of its eyes.

Fly repellent
A number of products are available to help keep flies off. Some are poured onto a cloth and wiped on the pony's coat. Some ponies do not mind spray products.

Coping with flies

Horses and ponies that suffer greatly from flies are best stabled in the daytime and turned out at night. If this is not possible, then fly fringes or fly masks, which cover most of the face, can help. Horses provide their own protection by standing in pairs nose to tail, each swishing the flies off the other's face.

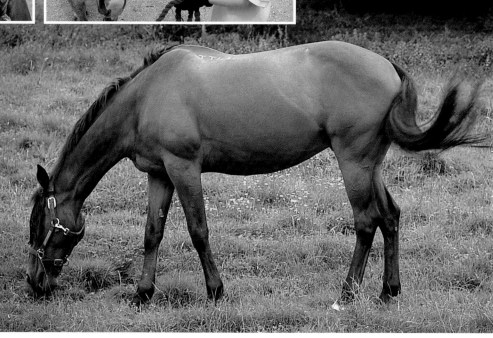

Leg and foot care

In the winter a horse's or pony's legs and feet need special attention. Constant exposure to wet and mud can cause cracks and soreness, called mud fever (page 57), that may become infected, so it is worth trying to protect them from this. Riding on ice is dangerous, but you can ride in snow if you grease its feet.

Leg greasing
Applying petroleum jelly to a horse's lower legs and heels helps protect them from the mud and wet.

Foot greasing
Putting grease in the hoof stops snow from getting inside it.

Keeping warm
A clipped horse or pony will stay warm in the coldest weather if it has sufficient food and if it wears a thick blanket. It is better to add an undersheet or another blanket for warmth than to shut the top half of a Dutch door.

Breaking the ice
In severe weather the water in pasture troughs and even in stalls will freeze. To ensure that your pony has enough to drink, you must break the ice several times a day. If possible, use warm water to fill up the troughs, because this will refreeze less quickly.

Essential winter care

Native ponies can live outdoors without blankets all winter if they have enough to eat. Depending on the weather, the pasture, the pony, and its work, it will need hay and possibly concentrated feed from midwinter to spring.

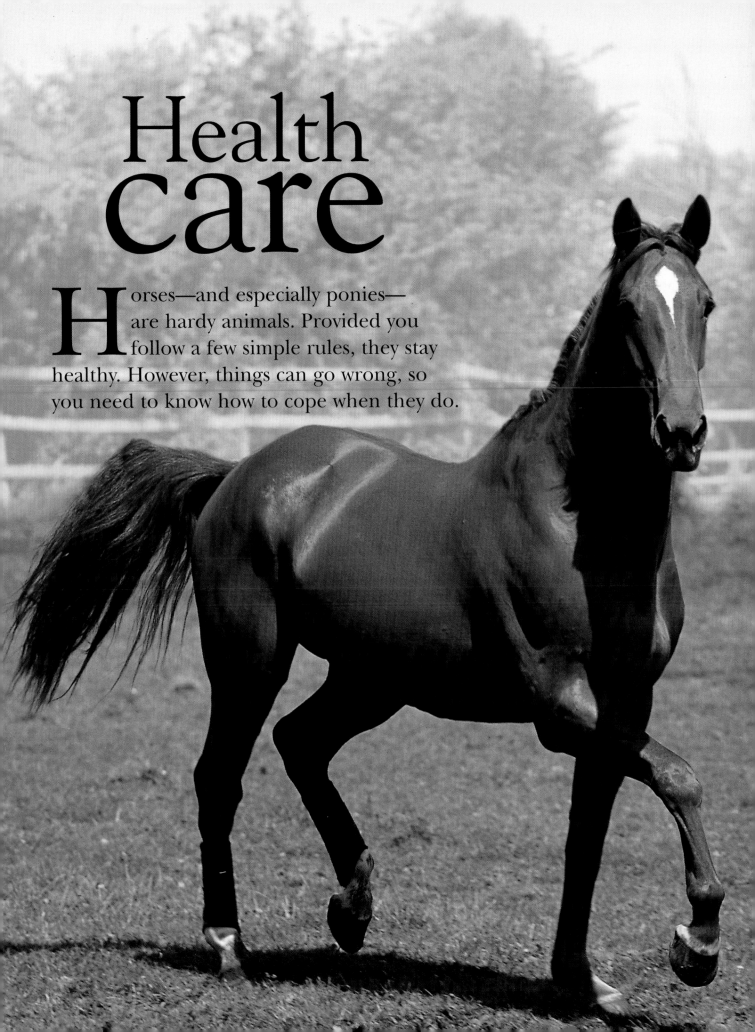

Health care

Horses—and especially ponies—are hardy animals. Provided you follow a few simple rules, they stay healthy. However, things can go wrong, so you need to know how to cope when they do.

Pricked ears
Although ears laid back are a sign of bad temper rather than sickness, pricked ears show that the pony is interested in what is happening. Its ears move to catch the slightest sound.

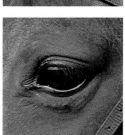

Bright eyes
A pony's eyes should be bright and clear. The pupils should dilate in the dark and contract in bright light. The eyes should not run, though a small amount of dirt may collect in the corners.

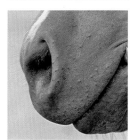

Dry nose
A horse's nose should be dry. Some animals that are allergic to dust may have a slight, watery nasal discharge. But thick mucus, especially if greenish or yellow, is a sign of infection.

Other things to check

A healthy horse or pony should be neither fat nor thin. Ribs sticking out and a pot belly are signs of worms, and so is a cough. The horse's breathing should be relaxed and regular—noisy breathing may be a sign of lung disease or dust allergies. When resting, the horse should feel warm with cool feet and legs. Its droppings should be firm balls and just break on reaching the ground.

Signs of good health

A healthy pony has bright eyes, a shiny coat, a hearty appetite, and is interested in everything that goes on around it. Ponies are inquisitive and will come and investigate what you are doing. In a pasture they stay together in a group. A pony that stays away from the others may not be well.

Signs of poor health

If a pony stands with its head down, looking unhappy; if its eyes are dull and its coat is in poor condition, it may be sick. Pinch its skin between your finger and thumb. It should spring straight back into place. If it does not, the pony may be dehydrated (lacking water):

Full of life

Although horses and ponies in a pasture spend most of the time grazing, they will play and gallop around, especially if they are young. This helps them exercise and also keeps them healthy. They only sleep for about four hours a day, and one always stands guard while the others lie down. Horses and ponies can also doze standing up.

Health routines

Regular worming and vaccinations are essential to help keep a horse or pony healthy. It is important to know your pony's usual pulse, temperature, and respiration (breathing) rates, and also to be able to recognize its normal behavior. Being aware of these things will help you find anything that is wrong and fix it quickly.

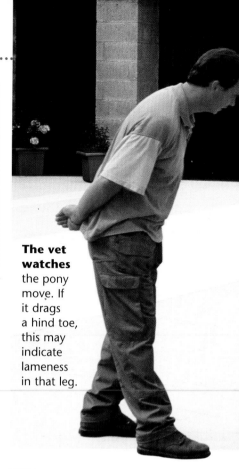

The vet watches the pony move. If it drags a hind toe, this may indicate lameness in that leg.

Checking the pulse and respiration

Feel for the pulse with your fingers just under the pony's jawbone. Count the number of beats you feel in one minute. It should be 35 to 45 when the pony is resting. The pony's respiration rate is 10 to 20 breaths a minute when resting.

Checking legs

A pony's legs should feel cool and be free from swelling. By running your hand down each leg one at a time every day, you will be able to feel any swelling or heat, which may indicate an injury even if the pony does not seem lame.

Trotting in hand is the easiest way to check for lameness.

Lameness

If you walk or trot a horse or pony on hard ground, such as concrete, it is possible for someone watching to tell on which leg it is lame. With foreleg lameness, a pony will nod its head as the sound front leg hits the ground.

Keep a firm hold of the thermometer for two minutes before you withdraw and read it. Make sure you do not let go!

Taking the temperature

If you think your pony may be sick, ask an adult to help you take its temperature. The normal temperature for a horse or pony is between 99–100°F. Grease the bulb of the thermometer and insert it gently into the pony's rectum.

Worming

Horses and ponies need to be wormed every four to eight weeks. The wormer may be a powder, which you sprinkle in your pony's food, or a paste, which is squirted onto its tongue with an applicator. Ponies don't seem to mind the taste. You should ask an adult to help you worm your pony.

Care of the teeth

Horses' and ponies' back teeth often wear unevenly, making the mouth uncomfortable. It is a good idea to have them checked each year by a vet or an equine dentist. He or she will rasp smooth any sharp edges, using a gag to keep the pony's mouth open and to avoid being bitten.

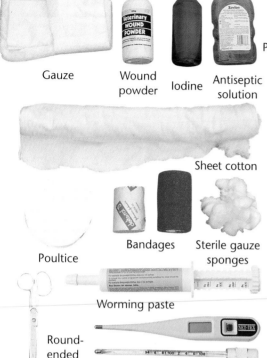

Gauze

Wound powder

Iodine

Antiseptic solution

Petroleum jelly

Sheet cotton

Poultice

Bandages

Sterile gauze sponges

Worming paste

Round-ended scissors

Thermometers

First aid

It is useful to know how to carry out basic first-aid routines to help you deal with a horse's or pony's minor injuries and problems yourself. But if a pony shows obvious signs of sickness, or is lame or badly injured, you should seek the advice of a knowledgeable adult, because it may be necessary to contact the vet. Prompt veterinary attention can prevent a problem from getting worse.

First-aid kit

It is a good idea to have a first-aid kit handy. Keep it in a clean, dry place, and check it from time to time. If you use any of the contents, replace them so they will be there the next time you need to use them in an emergency.

Be sure to use sterile gauze sponges.

Clean the wound from the center out.

Preventing infection

Thorough cleaning of a wound will prevent infection and help it heal quickly. Clip off the surrounding hair. Pour warm water into a clean container and add some antiseptic. Dip sterile gauze sponges into the solution, squeeze them out, and use them to clean the wound. Use more gauze sponges until the wound is clean. If the wound bleeds a lot, or is near a joint or tendon, call the vet.

Hosing the legs

Hosing down an injured leg with cold water can reduce swelling and pain. Ask a helper to hold the pony and just trickle the hose on its leg to start. Then hose down the leg for about 15 minutes, stop, let it warm up again, and then repeat the process once or twice more.

Leg bandages

Bandages may be used to hold a dressing in place, support injured or swollen legs, and keep cold, wet legs warm. Bandages are put over a layer of sheet cotton. When bandaging the legs, crouch—do not kneel—beside it.

Applying wound powder

You can treat minor cuts and scratches with antiseptic wound powder, which you sprinkle onto the wound after cleaning it. As well as helping to prevent infections, wound powder helps keep flies away.

1 Bandage any dressing, then wrap sheet cotton around the leg. Cover the coronet and make sure the cotton is kept flat.

2 Start applying the bandage just below the knee or hock. Hold the end in place until you have secured it with a few more turns.

1 Cut the poultice to the size you need, and soak it in either hot or cold water. Squeeze out the water while keeping the poultice flat.

2 Place the poultice over the sole of the pony's hoof and start to bandage it in place. It is easiest to use a stretchy, self-adhesive bandage.

3 Bandage in a figure-eight shape around the hoof. When you have finished, tape a thick cotton bandage or a bag around the hoof.

Finished poultice bandage

Soaking a foot

Soaking involves putting a horse's foot and lower leg in a low-sided, rubber bucket of warm water with Epsom salts. This is used to help draw out hoof infections. The horse needs to stand with its leg in the bucket for 10–15 minutes, preferably twice a day. Unless the horse is quiet, ask an adult to help.

Applying a poultice

Poultices may be used hot or cold. A hot poultice is used to draw out infection from a wound or abscess; a cold one to reduce swelling, for example, when the foot is bruised. You can buy chemically-prepared poultices made of cotton and gauze.

3 Work down the leg and over the fetlock and pastern until you reach the top of the hoof. Try to keep the tension even as you work.

4 When you reach the coronet, apply the bandage in the opposite direction and work your way back up the pony's leg.

5 By the time you reach the end of the bandage, you should have arrived back at the place on the leg where you began.

6 Secure the bandage with Velcro straps or tapes. Tie the tapes neatly on the inside or the outside of the pony's leg.

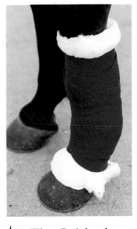

7 The finished bandage should be firm, but not too tight. You should be able to see a layer of sheet cotton at its top and bottom.

Common ailments

E ven the best-cared-for horse
or pony will occasionally suffer
from a minor ailment. Once you
can recognize what is wrong you
can carry out simple treatments.
Look for signs of abnormal
behavior in your pony, for areas
of sore, rubbed skin, for lumps
and swellings, and for any signs
of lameness. Laminitis and colic
are the most serious problems you
are likely to encounter. Both can
be caused by a pony overeating.

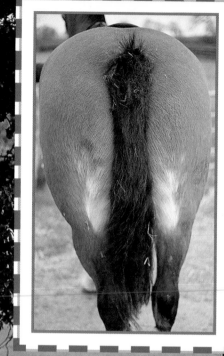

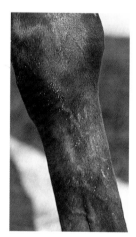

Botfly eggs

Little yellow specks on
a pony's lower legs in the
summer are botfly eggs.
Ask an adult to scrape
them off with a botfly
knife. If the pony licks the
eggs, bot larvae develop
in its mouth and stomach.
Worming with ivermectin
in the early winter destroys
the botfly larvae.

Rubbing mane

Even if they do not have sweet itch, many
horses and ponies rub their manes and tails in
the summer, which looks unpleasant and causes
soreness. Rub in medicated shampoo or lotion
or protect the horse with a special lightweight,
hooded blanket and a fly mask for the face.

Sweet itch

Sweet itch is the
name of an allergy from
the bites of biting midges,
which causes some ponies
to rub themselves raw
to try and get rid of the
irritation. The mane and
tail are usually affected.

The midges mostly bite
early in the morning and
at dusk, so the best way
to avoid sweet itch with a
susceptible pony is to keep
it in its stall at these times.

**Medicated shampoo
or lotion** from a vet or
tack shop rubbed into the
roots of the mane and tail
helps relieve sweet itch.

Looking for mites
You may not see the mites, which are tiny, but thick, brown wax in the ears gives them away.

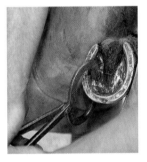

Problems with a pony's ears

Shaking of the head, rubbing of the ears, and a discharge from the ears are all signs of ear problems. The symptoms may simply be the result of ear mites (tiny parasites), but they could also indicate an infection. If you suspect something is wrong with a pony's ears, have them examined by a vet.

Symptoms of colic

Colic is a common digestive problem, and can be very serious. Affected ponies often roll, but then do not shake themselves afterward. They may lie down and get up again frequently. If badly affected, they will sweat and be in obvious pain. If you see signs of colic, call the vet immediately.

Mud fever
Sore, cracked heels need treatment by a vet.

Hoof testers
Check for laminitis by applying pressure.

Swollen leg
This swelling on the lower leg might be the result of a knock or a sprain. Hosing down the leg (page 54) may help.

Swellings in the legs

Swellings can be caused by ligament or tendon injuries, bruising, splints (bony enlargements), arthritis, and other conditions. They may feel hard or soft, there may be heat in the leg, and the pony may be lame. It is generally best to seek veterinary advice.

Mud fever and laminitis

Mud fever is a winter hoof ailment; ponies that eat too much rich, summer grass can get laminitis, a very painful inflammation of the hoof. It usually affects the front feet, which feel hot, and the pony may be lame. If a pony has symptoms of laminitis, get it in from the pasture and call the vet.

Caring for a sick pony

A sick or injured pony that is confined to its stall likes to follow its normal routine as much as possible. Provided the pony is not too ill, you can give it a light daily grooming. Keep it warm with blankets if necessary, and make sure it always has clean water to drink. If it cannot go out at all, pick the pony a few handfuls of grass to eat each day, as long as the vet allows it. Never feed a pony lawn cuttings.

Giving a pony medicine

Medicines come in different forms—powders, pills, and liquids. Powders and liquids can be mixed in the feed. Putting them in a tasty, moist food, such as applesauce, and mixing it into their feed helps disguise the taste. Pills can be crushed between two spoons and fed in the same way. Liquids may be dropped onto the horse's tongue or inside the lower lip, or squirted into the mouth with a syringe.

Hide a pill or capsule in an apple slice. Cut a slit in the apple and push the pill down into it so the pulp of the fruit surrounds the pill and masks the taste.

Powdered medicine can be sprinkled onto a slice of bread with molasses. Fold the bread to hide the powder and tear or cut it into bite-sized pieces.

Convalescence

A horse or pony confined to a stall for a long time gets very bored, especially when it is feeling better. Divide its hay ration into several smaller nets to keep it occupied. Visit the pony frequently, and bring treats with you. Some horses and ponies like a radio left on for company.

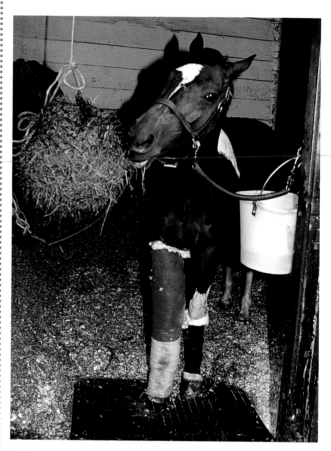

Things to play with

If the horse or pony is allowed to move around, it may enjoy playing with a horse ball. You can buy several types of horse toys, which are designed to be safe and impossible for the horse to puncture if it bites or kicks them.

Stable toys include hanging balls, on which you can smear molasses.

Feline friend

When a horse or pony has to be confined to its stall for long periods and it has no other equine friends around, it may appreciate the company of a friendly household cat or dog, especially if you cannot visit the pony as often as you would like.

Grazing on the lawn

If your pony cannot go out into the pasture, but is allowed out of its stall, spare a few minutes each day to give it some in-hand grazing, provided the vet allows it.

The road to recovery

Once the pony has recovered from its illness you have to get it strong before it can resume normal work. Start by giving it gentle exercise. A good way to do this is with a few minutes' in-hand walking each day, gradually increasing the time and distance. If you are leading the pony on a road, keep it to the side and walk in the direction of traffic. Position yourself between the pony and the traffic—even if it means you have to lead on the right side.

Wear a helmet and gloves when leading a pony on the road.

A pony should wear a bridle when being led on the road.

Wear light-colored or reflective clothing

Points of a horse

The points of a horse or pony are the visible parts of its anatomy. Each has a name, which you will find useful to learn because they will help you understand magazines and books you read and instructions you may be given when you take riding lessons. By becoming familiar with these terms, you will learn more about horses and ponies and be better able to talk to other people interested in horses. You will be able to talk about pony care and discuss any problems with a vet.

Conformation

Conformation means the way in which a horse or pony is put together. It varies according to type and breed, but the body should look in proportion. A small head; large, clear eyes; sloping shoulders and pasterns; a good circumference of bone below the knee; a short back, and powerful hindquarters are considered good conformation.

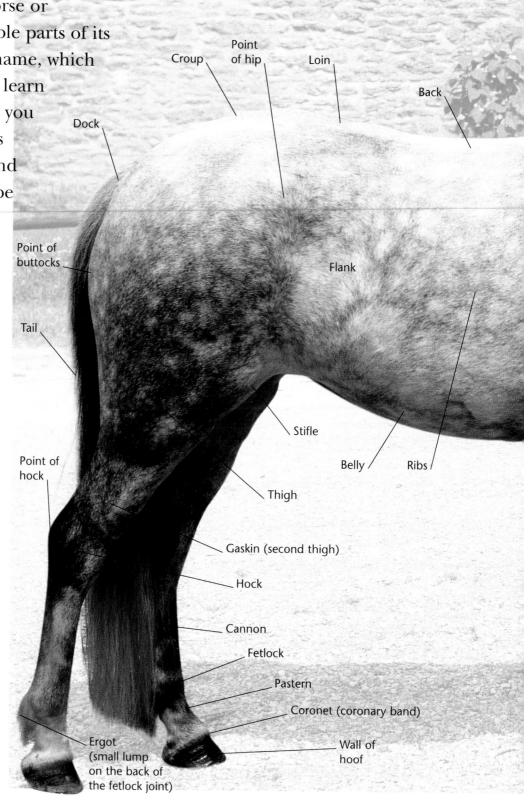

Croup
Point of hip
Loin
Back
Dock
Point of buttocks
Flank
Tail
Stifle
Belly
Ribs
Point of hock
Thigh
Gaskin (second thigh)
Hock
Cannon
Fetlock
Pastern
Coronet (coronary band)
Ergot (small lump on the back of the fetlock joint)
Wall of hoof

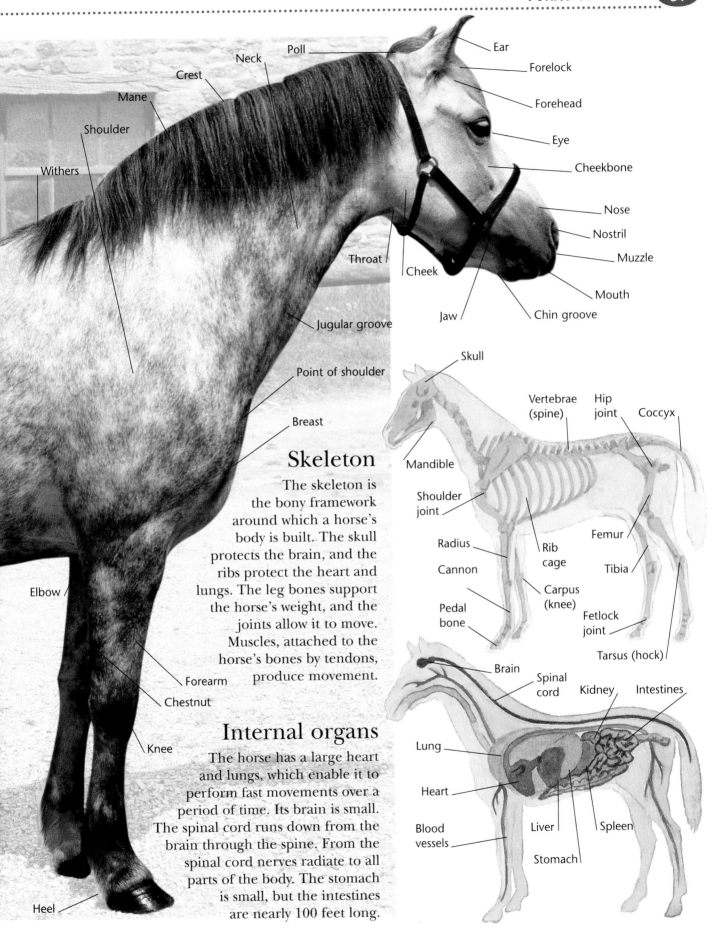

Poll
Neck
Crest
Mane
Shoulder
Withers
Ear
Forelock
Forehead
Eye
Cheekbone
Nose
Nostril
Muzzle
Throat
Cheek
Mouth
Jaw
Chin groove
Jugular groove
Point of shoulder
Breast
Elbow
Forearm
Chestnut
Knee
Heel

Skeleton

The skeleton is the bony framework around which a horse's body is built. The skull protects the brain, and the ribs protect the heart and lungs. The leg bones support the horse's weight, and the joints allow it to move. Muscles, attached to the horse's bones by tendons, produce movement.

Internal organs

The horse has a large heart and lungs, which enable it to perform fast movements over a period of time. Its brain is small. The spinal cord runs down from the brain through the spine. From the spinal cord nerves radiate to all parts of the body. The stomach is small, but the intestines are nearly 100 feet long.

Skull
Vertebrae (spine)
Hip joint
Coccyx
Mandible
Shoulder joint
Radius
Cannon
Rib cage
Femur
Pedal bone
Carpus (knee)
Tibia
Fetlock joint
Tarsus (hock)

Brain
Spinal cord
Kidney
Intestines
Lung
Heart
Blood vessels
Liver
Stomach
Spleen

Glossary

American barn

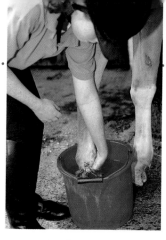

Soaking the foot

You may not understand all the words you come across as you read about horses and ponies and get to know more about their world. This list explains what some of them mean.

American barn A stable design used in the U.S. in which a large barn is divided into several **box stalls** on either side of a central aisle.

anvil A shaped iron block on which a **farrier** works metal to make horseshoes.

bit The part of a bridle that goes in a horse's mouth—usually made of steel.

boarding barn A stable where you pay to keep your horse on the premises. Some allow the owner to visit every day and do all the work; some have stable staff who carry out all the work involved.

body brush A short-bristled brush used for removing dirt and oil from a horse's or pony's coat.

box stall A stall in which a horse is free to move around.

braiding A pony's mane may be braided for a show.

bulk feeds Grass, hay, or other **forage** that forms the main part of a horse's diet.

cantle The back of a saddle.

cast When a horse or pony, lying in its stall, becomes wedged and is unable to move or get up.

chaps Leather leggings worn over pants to protect a **farrier**'s or rider's legs.

clenches The ends of horseshoe nails that are hammered down to hold a shoe in place.

clippers Hand-held machines with many small blades used for **clipping** a pony's coat.

clipping Removing a horse's or pony's winter coat to enable it to work without sweating excessively.

cob A short-legged, small, stocky horse, usually with a quiet temperament.

colic Abdominal pain. Colic can be very serious and needs veterinary attention.

concentrated feeds Corn, pellets, and sweet feeds fed to a horse in small quantities, as opposed to **bulk feeds**.

concentrates The grains such as oats and barley that make up **concentrated feeds**.

conformation The overall shape and proportions of a horse or pony.

coronet (coronary band) The part of a horse's leg immediately above the hoof.

curry comb a) A metal comb on a wooden handle used for cleaning a **body brush** when grooming. b) A plastic or rubber version that can be used on a horse or pony in a circular motion to remove mud and loose hairs.

dandy brush A wooden-backed brush with long, stiff bristles used for removing dried mud and for grooming a pasture-kept pony.

deep litter A system of stable management in which only the droppings are removed in daily mucking out and fresh bedding is placed on top of the old.

dock The area under the top of a horse's tail, and the top part of the tail itself.

eggbutt snaffle A snaffle **bit** in which the mouthpiece is joined to the rings by thickened, smooth pieces of metal to prevent the bit from pinching the corners of the pony's mouth.

farrier A professionally qualified person who shoes horses and trims their hooves.

fetlock The joint on the lower part of a horse's leg just above the hoof.

forage Food for a horse or pony, especially grass, hay, and **haylage**.

frog The V-shaped structure in the sole of a horse's foot that acts as a shock absorber.

fullered shoes Horseshoes that have a groove running around the underside to give a better grip.

girth a) The strap that goes around a horse's belly to hold the saddle in place. b) The part of the horse around which the girth fits.

grazing rotation Grazing a pasture with cattle and sheep after horses to even out the pasture and prevent the build-up of worm eggs.

halter A piece of equipment consisting of a noseband, headpiece, throatlash, and a strap that joins the throatlash to the noseband.

hands The units used to measure a horse's height. One hand equals 4 inches.

haylage Vacuum-packed, partly dried hay. It is dust-free and fed to horses with breathing problems.

horse An equine animal 14.3 **hands** (59 inches) high or taller.

in hand Leading a horse or pony while on foot.

kick bolt A foot-operated bolt on the bottom part of a stall door.

laminitis (Also known as founder) A painful inflammation of the inside of a horse's hooves, usually caused by overfeeding or food that is too rich.

lungeing Exercising a riderless horse on a long rein attached to a special **halter**. The horse is asked to walk, trot, and canter in a circle in both directions.

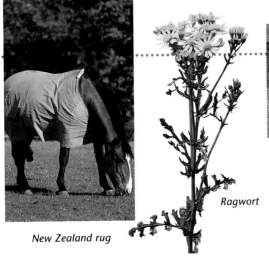

New Zealand rug

Ragwort

Clenches on a shod horse

Sweat scraper

Clippers for clipping a horse

manger A container, usually attached to a wall of a stall, in which the horse's food is placed.

martingale A piece of tack designed to stop a horse from tossing its head too high. A standing martingale runs from the noseband to the **girth**; a running martingale from the reins to the girth.

mowing a pasture Cutting down weeds and long, coarse grasses to improve grazing.

mud fever A condition in which the heels and lower legs get sore and cracked.

muzzle The area around a horse's mouth.

native pony A breed, like Exmoor, Welsh, or Highland, that was bred on the moors and mountains of Britain.

near side The left side of a horse or pony.

New Zealand rug A waterproof blanket, held on with special straps, worn by a pasture-kept horse.

off side The right side of a horse or pony.

pastern The part of a horse's leg between the foot and the **fetlock** joint.

pasture shelter An open-fronted shed in a pasture that provides horses and ponies with some protection from the weather.

pellets A balanced mix of prepared feed.

points a) The visible features of a horse. b) Areas on a horse that are described as part of its color.

pommel The front part of a saddle.

pony An equine animal up to 14.2 **hands** (58 inches) high.

poultice This is a dressing used to draw out heat and swelling from an injury, tightening the skin, and cooling the area around the injury.

pulling a mane and tail Pulling out long hairs to neaten the appearance.

quartering A quick brushing done before exercising a horse or pony.

quick-release knot A knot that can be undone quickly by pulling one end of the rope.

ragwort A yellow-flowered plant that is highly poisonous to horses and other animals.

roller A broad band that fastens around a horse's belly to hold a blanket in place.

rolling A horse or pony lying on its back with legs kicking in the air, rolling from side to side.

saddle pad A used under a saddle.

saddle soap A substance that cleans, nourishes, and preserves leather.

shavings Wood shavings usually dust-extracted and sold in vacuum-packed bales for animal bedding.

skip A container for shoveling droppings into when mucking out.

soaking a foot Soaking a horse's or pony's foot in a bucket containing a warm solution of Epsom salts to draw out infection.

stable stains Marks on a stabled horse caused by lying in dirty bedding.

studs Metal pieces screwed into the heels of a horse's shoes to prevent it from slipping.

surcingle A strap attached to a blanket to fasten it around a horse's belly.

sweat scraper Used for removing water from the horse's coat when washing it or sponging it down.

sweet feed A type of prepared **concentrated feed** in which various ingredients are mixed together.

sweet itch An allergic condition causing a horse to rub its mane and tail.

tack All the pieces of saddlery used on a riding horse or pony.

tail strap A strap across the back of a trailer that stops a horse from moving backward.

thatching Putting straw under a wet horse's blanket to help it dry without getting the blanket wet.

thoroughbred A breed of horse registered in the General Stud Book. All racehorses are registered thoroughbreds.

throatlash A strap on a bridle or **halter** that goes around a horse's throat.

trailer Horse carrier towed behind a vehicle. It may hold one or two horses. Some allow you to unload the horse from the front, but it is more common to have back unload doors.

turning out Letting a horse or pony out in a pasture.

vaccination An injection to protect a horse from diseases such as Equine Infectious Anemia and tetanus.

van A vehicle used for transporting horses and ponies from place to place.

water brush A short-bristled brush used damp to lay the mane and tail in place when grooming.

weigh tape A tape wrapped around a horse's **girth** from which you can read off its weight.

withers The bony ridge at the base of a horse's neck.

worming Giving medicine to kill parasitic worms inside a horse's or pony's intestines.

Index

HORSE AND PONY WEBSITES
www.ponyclub.org
(official U.S. Pony Club website)
www.youngrider.com
(links to other horse and pony websites)
www.newrider.com
(advice and information for new riders)
www.ilph.org
(International League for the Protection of Horses website)

Kingfisher would like to thank: Everybody at **The Talland School of Equitation**, especially the Hutton family and Patricia Curtis. Everybody at **Hartpury College Equestrian Centre**, especially Margaret Linington-Payne. Models: Tom Alexander, Anna Bird, Emily Brady, James Cole, Emily Coles, Patricia Curtis, Sam Drinkwater, Amelia Ebanks, Naomi Ebanks, Helen Grundy, Sarah Grundy, Simon Grundy, Emma Harford, Brian Hutton, Sophie Kuropatwa, Thomas McEwen, Alasdair Nicol, Andrew Poynton (farrier), Max Thomas (farrier), Camilla Tracey, Ayako Watanabe, Laura Wilks and Sawako Yoshii. Also, many thanks to Lesley Ward.